Executive Wine Education

R. Sean Cochran

CONTENTS

CHAPTER 1

WHY DO EXECUTIVES NEED WINE EDUCATION?

I have a confession to share with you. I am not a wine expert. This may seem to be an interesting way to start a book about wine education, but the key focus of this book is on *executives*. I am a corporate executive.

I am currently a Managing Director in a global financial institution. I have spent the last 15 years of my life advising wealthy clients in the US, Europe and Asia on the investment of their financial assets and I coach and manage other client-facing professionals who carry similar roles. This career history does not make me a wine expert, but of course it does make me a corporate executive and this book is written for fellow corporate executives and for students preparing to enter the corporate world.

I have had an appreciation of wine for many years and as I have progressed in my professional career I have increasingly realized that wine knowledge is *professionally* relevant and not simply *personally* relevant. In 2004 I decided to take my interest in wine further and I became a Certified Specialist of Wine (CSW) through studies with the Society of Wine Educators and from that point onward I began to see wine knowledge in a different light. In a professional context a certain degree of wine knowledge can be useful, making this topic more than simply an interesting hobby. There are certain key essentials that any executive really should know about wine.

Generally speaking, there are many basic "essentials" that executives need to refine in order to operate in a professional context. An executive must understand how to dress formally (or at least appropriate to one's profession), how to shake hands properly, how to dine with proper etiquette, and how to interact comfortably in certain social contexts. This understanding is not acquired as an investment in fashion, food, or socializing. These are the elements of professional etiquette that an executive typically needs to master in order to move forward, and upward, in corporate life. This need for refinement and professional etiquette is particularly acute for client-facing and sales functions, but it is fundamental to a wide variety of professional roles. A certain level of wine fluency is a skill set that should be added to this list of essentials when it comes to executive refinement.

I would argue that this information, a fundamental understanding of wine, constitutes a class that *business* (as opposed to culinary) school should teach. It represents information that could very reasonably have been offered as *executive* education through your company, though I am sure it is not in the curriculum.

Throughout your professional career you will invariably come into contact with wine. This is true even if you don't care for wine. This is true even if you do not drink at all. You will attend client dinners, corporate functions, cocktail parties, and other events where wine is present. With a degree of wine knowledge you gain opportunities to connect, build rapport, and share common understanding. You become confident in ordering wine and pairing wine with food, and you can comfortably "join the conversation" on this subject. Without this knowledge you open yourself up to etiquette mistakes and you lose opportunities to connect. For many individuals (and countries) wine is intertwined with culture and understanding this connection can draw you immediately into conversations close to the heart. I've experienced this many times and it can be a powerful tool for connecting and building rapport.

Let me tell you a story to bring this into focus.

A very important client is coming to town tonight and you intend to take him to dinner. You spent the day going through your preparations and you invest time in ensuring that the odds of a successful evening are stacked in your favor. Your suit is elegant, your shoes are shined and your cufflinks are selected. You understand this basic etiquette very well.

You are waiting outside the restaurant and your client pulls up and gets out of his car. He walks up to greet you and you give a firm handshake and exchange small talk casually as you enter the restaurant. You understand the etiquette of such social exchanges.

You sit down at the table and your client tells you that he is in the mood for Bordeaux. *Do you know what that means?*

The waiter hands you the wine list because you are the host, but you notice that they do not serve Bordeaux wines. *Do you know how to substitute?*

Your client then indicates that he has changed his mind because he has decided to have the fish. *Why is having the fish relevant to his changing his mind about drinking Bordeaux?*

Your client then indicates that he grew up in New Zealand and would love for you to pick a wine from New Zealand. As you look over the wine list, *are you familiar with the iconic bottles of this region?*

In this situation a natural reaction is to simply indicate that you are not knowledgeable about wine and you may ask the server (or sommelier) to select something suitable. But could this have gone differently had you known a bit of essential information? *Yes.*

These are lost opportunities to demonstrate that you speak a common language. These are lost opportunities to build rapport through common understanding of an aspect of culture close to your client's heart. These are unfortunately also opportunities for you to expose certain etiquette gaps. And the evening has just begun.

I do not suggest that executives need to become sommeliers or Certified Specialists of Wine. I do assert that executives need to understand the essentials of wine.

What are the essentials?

For an executive, the "essentials" of wine entail an understanding of:
- The grapes used in certain key wine regions
- The aromas and flavors typical of these regions and grapes
- A comfort level in pairing wine with food
- Recognition of certain iconic wines which many of your clients and colleagues will recognize

That's it.

As you read on you will see that this book is organized in this prescribed manner and it does not aim to satisfy an academic interest in the varying nuances of wine. This is not essential from an executive's perspective and I am the wrong author for such a book in any case.

Note that if you would like to supplement your reading with videos that trace these same topics you can do so for free by visiting www.executivewineeducation.com. Here you will find brief videos to accompany each of the chapters in this book and by combining the written chapter with the respective video you will enhance your learning experience. After each chapter you will notice a link to the website together with the title of the relevant video for your convenience.

While this book is primarily intended to support your professional education, I hope that it serves to raise your personal enjoyment and appreciation of wine as well.

Video Supplement: "Why Do Executives Need Wine Education?"
www.executivewineeducation.com

Enter the video title in the search window to access the free video.

CHAPTER 2

FRANCE

EXECUTIVE ESSENTIALS: BORDEAUX

By reputation, France is the most important winemaking country in the world and Bordeaux is arguably the most important wine region in France. When it comes to Bordeaux, you should avoid being overwhelmed and we will zero in on some of the essentials.

It will help if you mentally divide Bordeaux into 3 sub-regions for simplicity, namely the **Left Bank**, the **Right Bank**, and **Sauternes**. The Left Bank and Right Bank areas are known for red wines and Sauternes is known for its sweet white wines.

Cabernet Sauvignon and **Merlot** are the two red grapes in particular that have the greatest international reputation, though there are actually 5 different grapes that can potentially form the red Bordeaux blend in the Left Bank and Right Bank areas.

In the Sauternes region they allow a particular rot, known as **"Noble Rot"** (formally botrytis cineria), to attack the grapes, and without the presence of this rot they cannot make this famous sweet white wine.

BORDEAUX GEOGRAPHY

The overall Bordeaux region is located in Southern France and is situated around the Gironde River estuary, which is fed by the confluence of two rivers, namely the Garonne and the Dordogne. The area to the south of the Gironde is known as the "Left Bank" and the area to the north of the Gironde (and Dordogne) river is known as the "Right Bank". Both the Right Bank and the Left Bank are home to some of the most famous red wines in the world.

Sauternes is located further south and upriver along the Garonne River and it is here that the famous Sauternes white dessert wine is produced.

BORDEAUX GRAPES

Both the Left Bank and Right Bank center around the **5 traditional Bordeaux red grapes**: Cabernet Sauvignon, Merlot, Cabernet Franc, Petit Verdot, and Malbec. If someone refers to a "Bordeaux blend" they are referring to wines blended from these 5 grapes.

Cabernet Sauvignon and **Merlot** tend to share the leading role with the other grapes bringing different characteristics to the blend as the supporting cast. It is fair to say that the Cabernet Sauvignon and Merlot wines of the rest of the world are often aspiring to the heights of Bordeaux, the home of these noble grapes.

The Left Bank area tends to focus more on Cabernet Sauvignon as the driving element of their wines whereas the Right Bank focuses more on Merlot.

The region of Sauternes focuses primarily on the **Semillon** grape, but the leading role in the region is actually played by a particular type of rot, formally known as botrytis cinerea (aka, "noble rot"). To create the famous dessert wine of Sauternes they allow this rot to attack the fruit which raises the sugar level in the affected grapes before they are pressed and fermented. This leads to a final product which is sweet and complex and which can grow in complexity as it ages in the bottle.

CABERNET SAUVIGNON (LEFT BANK) TASTING NOTES

Cabernet Sauvignon drives the blend in the Left Bank Bordeaux wines. If you like Cabernet Sauvignon wines then you will likewise be fond of Left Bank Bordeaux. In fact, it is fair to say that the Left Bank is home to the most famous Cabernet Sauvignon wines in the world.

Typical **Cabernet Sauvignon** (Left Bank) aromas, flavors, and characteristics:
- Red currant, cherry, bell pepper
- Cedar, tobacco, dust
- Vanilla
- High tannin levels
- Dark color

Cabernet Sauvignon wines are known for their firm tannin structure, robust flavors and aromas, and dark color. This can be very serious wine and many of the major wine regions of the world try their hand in producing it. The Left Bank reigns supreme in this very competitive category.

CABERNET SAUVIGNON (LEFT BANK) FOOD PAIRING

Potential food pairings for **Cabernet Sauvignon** (Left Bank) wine:
- Beef, lamb, grilled meat
- Stews
- Rich red sauces
- Bay and rosemary

The full-bodied, tannic wines of the Left Bank are a good match for full-flavored foods. Wines that are high in tannin also tend to be a good match for foods higher in fat content. Red meat and rich sauces come to mind as good matches for this wine.

CABERNET SAUVIGNON (LEFT BANK) BOTTLES TO KNOW

There are many iconic wines from the Left Bank. As an executive you should have an understanding of a few of these winemakers and their importance. Certain Left Bank Bordeaux winemakers (known as "Chateaux") even have an active futures market in their wines for investors hoping to invest in the bottles before they are even available. The good news is that the important Chateaux for you to know do not tend to change year-in, year-out. The important Chateaux have been important for over 100 years.

In 1855 Napolean III requested a classification of Bordeaux wines in advance of the Universal Exhibition in Paris and the criteria was simply the price (as a proxy for quality) at that time. This classification (focused on Left Bank wines) has since become known as the **"Bordeaux Classification of 1855"** and it divided Bordeaux into 5 categories known as "growths". The top category is referred to as "first-growth Bordeaux" followed by "second-growth" and so on through "fifth-growth". This categorization was established in 1855 and has only been amended one time since when Chateau Mouton Rothschild was elevated from second-growth to first-growth status.

The 5 First-Growth Bordeaux wines:
- Chateau Haut-Brion
- Chateau Lafite-Rothschild
- Chateau Latour
- Chateau Margaux
- Chateau Mouton Rothschild

These are legends and highly collectable. As an executive, these are the Left Bank Bordeaux bottles that you need to recognize.

MERLOT (RIGHT BANK) TASTING NOTES

When you think of the Right Bank, think of Merlot. The Right Bank is able to use all 5 Bordeaux grape varieties in varying proportion, though it tends to have Merlot-driven blends.

Typical **Merlot** (Right Bank) aromas, flavors, and characteristics:
- Plum, cherry, prune, bell pepper
- Chocolate
- Vanilla
- Medium tannin structure
- Dark color

Right Bank (Merlot-driven) wines are often made in a style very similar to Left Bank (Cabernet-driven) wines, but they do tend to be a bit softer in tannin structure and sometimes slightly less powerful and robust than their Cabernet Sauvignon dominated counterparts.

MERLOT (RIGHT BANK) FOOD PAIRING

Potential food pairings for **Merlot** (Right Bank) wine:
- Grilled meat, hamburger
- Grilled tuna
- Red sauce, meat sauce
- Basil, thyme

Many of the food pairings that work for Left Bank wines would work for Right Bank wines as well, but you should expect a slightly less forceful wine from the Right Bank with a somewhat softer tannin structure. This, of course, can vary by Chateau as each is able to blend the Bordeaux grapes in slightly different proportions.

MERLOT (RIGHT BANK) BOTTLES TO KNOW

The Right Bank wines were *not* included in the Bordeaux Classification of 1855 and therefore do not have assigned "growths", but some bottles are nonetheless world-renowned and on equal footing with the first-growths of the Left Bank. As an executive, you should know these Right Bank bottles in particular.

Chateau Petrus

Chateau Petrus is the most famous Merlot wine in the world and every bit as expensive and collectable as the first-growth Bordeaux wines from the Left Bank. This wine is a legend.

Chateau Cheval Blanc

This is a very famous wine and was actually the trophy wine for one of the main characters in the movie "Sideways". Merlot is an important part of this wine's blend but it is actually dominated by Cabernet Franc, another of the 5 Bordeaux grapes. It is important to recognize this wine in the context of famous Right Bank wines, but it is also interesting to note that it is the most famous example of Cabernet Franc (blended with Merlot), a grape that typically plays a supporting role to the other Bordeaux grapes.

SAUTERNES TASTING NOTES

Typical **Sauternes** aromas, flavors, and characteristics:
- Pineapple, apricot, peach
- Honey
- Vanilla
- Thick texture and mouthfeel
- Golden color

Sauternes is made primarily using the Semillon grape but the defining feature of the flavor profile of this wine is not due to the grapes at all but rather to its reliance on the "noble rot". "Noble rot" (known formally as botrytis cinerea) must attack the grapes in order to raise the sugar levels to support the creation of these wines. If the rot is not present, then they cannot make these wines. This method of winemaking creates highly complex sweet white wines which can age and increase in complexity over time.

SAUTERNES FOOD PAIRING

Potential food pairings for **Sauternes**:
- Foie gras
- Crème brulee
- Fruits

Sauternes can be used to accompany dessert and fruit, but it's best known pairing is together with Foie gras (duck liver). Foie gras is a rich delicacy and the pairing with Sauternes is a perfect, and very well known, match.

SAUTERNES BOTTLES TO KNOW

Chateau d'Yquem
Most white (or sweet) wines do not materially benefit from bottle aging, but that is not the case for Sauternes which is known to develop meaningfully over time in the bottle. Sauternes can form part of many collectors' wine cellars for this reason and the most famous chateau in Sauternes is the world-famous Chateau d'Yquem. Bottles of Chateau d'Yquem fetch extremely high prices, are long-aging, and are well known globally.

EXECUTIVE SUMMARY: BORDEAUX

France is legendary for its winemaking history overall and Bordeaux in particular is one of its shining stars. Its reputation revolves around red wines and in particular its Cabernet and Merlot driven blends. Bordeaux is also known for a very famous sweet wine from the sub-region of Sauternes. In terms of iconic bottles to know, Bordeaux winemakers also top the list of the world's most collectable wines and you should recognize these important chateaux.

Video Supplement: "Bordeaux Essentials"
www.executivewineeducation.com

Enter the video title in the search window to access the free video.

EXECUTIVE ESSENTIALS: BURGUNDY

Burgundy is another of France's legendary wine regions, but its grapes and wines are quite different from Bordeaux. By far, the most important thing for an executive to remember about Burgundy is that it is the home to red wines from the **Pinot Noir** grape.

Beaujolais is another sub-region of Burgundy which is known for its soft, playful red wines made from the **Gamay** grape.

Finally Burgundy is also known for a sub-region called **Chablis** which produces high quality white wines from the **Chardonnay** grape.

BURGUNDY GEOGRAPHY

In terms of geography, the overall Burgundy region is inland and located in Eastern France. Chablis is the northernmost sub-region of Burgundy and Beaujolais is situated at the southern end of the region. The rest of Burgundy in between is where the famous Pinot Noir wines of Burgundy are produced.

BURGUNDY GRAPES

Burgundy is nearly synonymous with the **Pinot Noir** grape. If someone refers simply to "Burgundy" you can assume they are referring to Burgundy's Pinot Noir wines. Pinot Noir is a red grape grown all over the world but it traces its roots back to Burgundy. It is a notoriously challenging grape to grow, but is capable of creating very complex and aromatic red wines.

Beaujolais to the south of the main area of Burgundy is known for wines made from the **Gamay** grape. The Gamay grape is used to make light, fruity, and easy drinking red wines some of which are produced very quickly after harvest.

Chablis, to the north, is known for **Chardonnay** wines. Chardonnay is a grape that can show many different characteristics depending on how it is handled by the winemaker.

PINOT NOIR (BURGUNDY) TASTING NOTES

Typical **Pinot Noir** (Burgundy) aromas, flavors, and characteristics:
- Raspberries, cherries, blackberries, violets
- Earth
- Cinnamon, cloves
- Softer tannin structure
- Lighter color
- Soft mouth-feel and velvety texture

Note that Pinot Noir can be made in different styles. Some are fruitier, simpler wines and some are earthier and more full-bodied with highly complex aromas and flavor profiles.

PINOT NOIR (BURGUNDY) FOOD PAIRING

Potential food pairings for **Pinot Noir** (Burgundy):
- Duck, lamb, pork
- Grilled tuna, paella
- Mushrooms
- Red sauces
- Basil

Pinot Noir (Burgundy) is interesting in that it can be a "cross-over" wine that is able to be served with either meat or fish. Its tannin structure is typically softer than that of full-bodied red wine and its flavors and aromas are more delicate as well. Full-bodied red wines will tend to overpower and overwhelm fish whereas Pinot Noir may not. Lighter fish dishes would still be best served with a white wine, but Pinot Noir could work well with grilled tuna, for example.

BURGUNDY BOTTLES TO KNOW

Domaine de la Romanee Conti
Much like certain of the first-growth Bordeaux wines we've covered in the previous section, this wine is legendary. It is decidedly the most famous Pinot Noir wine in the world. Note that in conversation its name is often shortened to "DRC" rather than the full "Domain de la Romanee Conti". It is a collectable, prestigious wine and tends to be one of the most expensive bottles in the world as well.

GAMAY (BEAUJOLAIS) TASTING NOTES

Typical **Gamay** (Beaujolais) aromas, flavors, and characteristics:
- Banana, strawberry
- Violets, roses
- Perfume
- Very soft tannin structure

This is typically a light, easy-drinking wine, though it can also be made in a style similar to earthier Pinot Noirs. The lightest and fruitiest version of this region's wine is known as "Beaujolais Nouveau" which is fermented very quickly and released into the market each year on the 3rd Thursday of November.

In executive circles Beaujolais Nouveau may be derided as too simple and unsophisticated, but this perspective misses the fact that the wine has its place. It is interesting to see what wine tastes like when it is this young and for many observers it is a means of gauging the year's harvest since it is the first wine from the vineyards to hit the shelves. In this respect it is like a "leading indicator" for the potential of other wines as well.

GAMAY (BEAUJOLAIS) FOOD PAIRING

Potential food pairings for **Gamay** (Beaujolais):
- Roast turkey
- Pasta, pizza
- Salads, cheeses

This would make a nice picnic wine. You may consider serving this wine at a relatively cool temperature much as you would a white wine.

GAMAY (BEAUJOLAIS) BOTTLES TO KNOW

Georges DuBoeuf
This winemaker is a fairly ubiquitous producer of Beaujolais and the largest producer of Beaujolais Nouveau. If you would like to taste Beaujolais Nouveau in a given year there are invariably events and "release parties" to celebrate this event on the 3rd Thursday of November and Georges DuBoeuf wines will likely be present.

CHARDONNAY (CHABLIS) TASTING NOTES

Typical **Chardonnay** (Chablis) aromas, flavors, and characteristics:
- Green apple, grapefruit
- Butter, nuts
- Minerals, flint

There is a common distinction drawn between "old world" Chardonnay (Chablis, for example) and "new world" Chardonnay (from California, for example) in terms of characteristics. The difference is largely a function of winemaking style rather than fundamental differences in the fruit. In "old world" Chardonnay, such as Chablis, the wine is often not aged in oak and carries characteristic mineral notes. "New world" Chardonnay tends to be aged in oak which imparts vanilla and oak flavors.

CHARDONNAY (CHABLIS) FOOD PAIRING

Potential food pairings for **Chardonnay** (Chablis):
- Chicken, pork, veal
- Grilled fish, shellfish
- Butter, parsley

Chardonnay is often a more full-bodied wine as compared to other dry white wines. Chablis will tend to be lighter than Chardonnay from so-called "new world" regions such as California, but relatively full-bodied for a white wine nonetheless. As such it is a nice pairing for white meat.

CHARDONNAY (CHABLIS) BOTTLES TO KNOW

Grand Cru
There is one large Grand Cru vineyard area in Chablis, designating the finest vineyards in the region. This plot is subdivided into 7 smaller vineyard plots and the wines of these Grand Cru vineyards are high quality examples of Chablis.

EXECUTIVE SUMMARY: BURGUNDY

Burgundy is nearly synonymous with Pinot Noir red wines, and these wines have a cult-like following amongst certain wine enthusiasts. They are very distinctive, very aromatic, and can be very complex, particularly when made in the earthier style often associated with fine French Burgundy. Domaine de la Romanee Conti is the most famous example of such wine.

Burgundy is also home to Chablis in the north of the region and Beaujolais to the south. Chablis is known for Chardonnay white wines, whereas Beaujolais is known for soft, easy drinking red wines made from the Gamay grape. The Beaujolais region is also known for Beaujolais Nouveau, a red wine made for drinking shortly after harvest.

Video Supplement: "Burgundy Essentials"
www.executivewineeducation.com

Enter the video title in the search window to access the free video.

EXECUTIVE ESSENTIALS: RHONE

The Rhone region can be divided into the sub-regions of **Northern Rhone** and **Southern Rhone**. It is important for you to remember that the Northern Rhone is known as being home to red wines from the **Syrah** grape whereas the Southern Rhone creates red wines blending many different grapes together. Though the Rhone region's reputation is founded on red wines, most notably Syrah, it does also produce high quality and very aromatic white wines from the **Viognier** grape as well.

RHONE GEOGRAPHY

The Rhone region is in Southeast France and is situated around the Rhone River Valley. Just north of the Rhone region is Burgundy, and just south of the Rhone region is the region of Provence.

RHONE GRAPES

The Rhone is known primarily for being the cradle of **Syrah**, a red wine grape which is widely grown throughout the world and also goes by the name "Shiraz" in Australia. Note that the Syrah grape is actually *not* the same as the Petite Sirah grape which carries a seemingly similar name. The Syrah grape is grown throughout the Rhone Valley though most notably in Northern Rhone in particular.

In the Southern Rhone winemakers blend Syrah together with a wide variety of grapes. In fact, the red wines of the Southern Rhone are able to blend more than 20 different grapes to make their red wines, including white wine grapes which is unusual. In addition to Syrah, the **Grenache** grape tends to play a dominant role in many of the Southern Rhone wines.

In terms of white Rhone wines, you should be aware of the **Viognier** grape. This grape grows throughout the Rhone valley but its finest examples are from the sub-region of Condrieu within Northern Rhone.

SYRAH (NORTHERN RHONE) TASTING NOTES

Typical **Syrah** (Northern Rhone) aromas, flavors, and characteristics:
- Raspberry, jam, tar, musk
- Chocolate, smoke, black pepper
- Rosemary, lavender
- High tannin
- High alcohol levels
- Dark color

Syrah wines from the Rhone tend to have different characteristics than Syrah ("Shiraz") grown in Australia. Syrah from the Rhone is characteristically "smokey" and "peppery", whereas Syrah ("Shiraz") grown in Australia often tends to be "jammier", showing more fruit.

SYRAH (NORTHERN RHONE) FOOD PAIRING

Potential food pairings for **Syrah** (Northern Rhone) wine:
- Lamb, sausage, grilled meat
- Peppery sauces
- Pungent herbs and spices

Syrah is full-bodied and robust and can pair well with flavorful food and strong, or peppery, sauces.

SYRAH (NORTHERN RHONE) BOTTLES TO KNOW

Cote Rotie
The Cote Rotie sub-region of Northern Rhone is well known for quality Syrah wines. It is interesting to note that the winemakers in Cote Rotie are actually permitted to blend up to 20% Viognier (a white grape) together with Syrah (a red grape) in making their red wines. This enhances the aromas and is a practice which is atypical in red wine production elsewhere.

Guigal and the "La-La" Vineyards
Guigal is a well known winemaker in the Rhone having established a strong international reputation for the quality of their Cote Rotie wines. In particular Guigal is known for 3 different single-vineyard wines, namely La Mouline, La Landonne and La Turque. These wines are collectively often referred to as the "La-La" wines and are the most prized Rhone wines and in turn command very high prices.

GRENACHE (SOUTHERN RHONE) TASTING NOTES

Typical **Grenache** (Southern Rhone) aromas, flavors, and characteristics:
- Sour cherry, cranberry
- Violets
- High alcohol content
- Lighter color
- Low tannin levels

Grenache is more common as a blending grape than as a standalone wine and can be used to raise the alcohol content in the overall blend. The Southern Rhone wines blend many different grapes, but Grenache often occupies a large proportion of these blends.

GRENACHE (SOUTHERN RHONE) FOOD PAIRING

Potential food pairings for **Grenache** (Southern Rhone) wine:
- Slow cooked stew, roast lamb
- Game birds, turkey
- Tomato based sauces

Grenache tends to be relatively low in tannin and thus would not be an ideal pairing with certain high-fat high-flavor grilled meats or steaks. It would however go nicely with a slow cooked stew, for example.

GRENACHE (SOUTHERN RHONE) BOTTLES TO KNOW

Chateuneuf-du-Pape
This sub-region can include up to 13 different grapes in their blend, including the white grape Viognier. However, the wines tend to be predominantly Grenache within this blend.

VIOGNIER TASTING NOTES

Typical **Viognier** aromas, flavors, and characteristics:
- Passionfruit, peach, guava, honeysuckle
- Ginger, grass
- Extremely aromatic

This wine is best known for its aromas and it can come across like tropical fruit and a bottle of perfume combined.

VIOGNIER FOOD PAIRING

Potential food pairings for **Viognier** wine:
- Thai, Indian, and Moroccan dishes
- Shellfish and lobster
- Cheeses

Given its extraordinarily aromatic qualities, Viognier is a good pairing for dishes that are also aromatic in terms of their spices.

VIOGNIER BOTTLES TO KNOW

Condrieu
This sub-region is located in the northern tip of the Rhone and produces the world's finest Viognier wines.

EXECUTIVE SUMMARY: RHONE

The Rhone is best known for Syrah red wines in the Northern Rhone and Grenache-driven red wine blends in Southern Rhone. It is also known for being home to the highly aromatic Viognier wines of Condrieu.

Video Supplement: "Rhone Essentials"
www.executivewineeducation.com

Enter the video title in the search window to access the free video.

EXECUTIVE ESSENTIALS: CHAMPAGNE

When you think of Champagne, images of celebration naturally come to mind and the uncorking of sparkling wine is a common way to commemorate joyful events. However, it's important to bear in mind that Champagne and sparkling wine are not synonymous. Champagne is sparkling wine, but **not all sparkling wine is Champagne**. In order for a wine to be "Champagne" it must be the sparkling wine from the region of Champagne in France.

Another important point to bear in mind is the distinction between "vintage" and "non-vintage" Champagne. **"Vintage" Champagne** denotes Champagne that has been created from grapes grown solely in a single vintage year. "Non-vintage" Champagne denotes a blend of grapes potentially grown in several different years which are mixed together in order to produce a consistent house style. The creation of a consistent house style is common in Champagne through careful blending when the base wine of Champagne is created. The Champagne base wine is first fermented before a *second* fermentation is triggered in the bottles and which results in the characteristic carbonation in Champagne. "Vintage" Champagne is only produced in exceptional years using solely the fruit from that single year.

CHAMPAGNE GEOGRAPHY

Champagne is located in the North of France near and around the cities of Reims and Epernay.

CHAMPAGNE GRAPES

Champagne is made from the **Chardonnay, Pinot Noir**, and **Pinot Meunier** grapes. Chardonnay is a white grape whereas Pinot Noir and Pinot Meunier are both red grapes. An interesting fact about Champagne is that the winemakers very often produce colorless champagne from both red and white grapes and do so by simply discarding the skins of the red grapes before the pigment in the skins is able to color the wine. For example, the French Champagne term "blanc de blancs" translates literally as "white from whites" and indicates white champagne produced from white grapes. "Blanc de noirs" translates literally as "white from blacks" indicating white Champagne made from the red grapes Pinot Noir and Pinot Meunier.

CHAMPAGNE TASTING NOTES

Typical **Champagne** aromas, flavors, and characteristics:
- Apple, pear, citrus
- Nuts
- Yeast, toast
- High acidity

CHAMPAGNE FOOD PAIRING

Potential food pairings for **Champagne**:
- Shrimp and shellfish
- Brie and gouda cheeses
- Raspberries, strawberries
- Buttered popcorn

Champagne goes well with fruit, and its acidity and carbonation allow it to cut through the fat in foods like buttered popcorn which is also a very good match.

CHAMPAGNE BOTTLES TO KNOW

Dom Perignon
Dom Perignon is a vintage Champagne from the house of Moet et Chandon and is one of the most recognizable bottles in the world. It is named after a Benedictine Monk of the same name who is credited for many innovations in Champagne (though he did not discover the process of creating sparkling wine as is popularly believed).

Cristal
Cristal is a vintage Champagne from the house of Louis Roederer. It is known for its distinctive clear bottle with a flat bottom, and of course its high price.

EXECUTIVE SUMMARY: CHAMPAGNE

Champagne goes hand in hand with celebration and commemoration. Champagne is often a term casually assigned to all sparkling wine, but it actually only accurately refers to the sparkling wine of the Champagne region in Northern France. So-called "vintage" Champagnes are those made entirely from grapes harvested in a single given year, whereas it is otherwise very common for Champagne to blend juice from fruit grown in varying years in order to create a consistent house style. Famous Champagne houses (winemakers) that any executive should be familiar with are Moet et Chandon (maker of Dom Perignon) and Louis Roederer (maker of Cristal), both of which would make very suitable bottles to commemorate important events.

Video Supplement: "Champagne Essentials"
www.executivewineeducation.com

Enter the video title in the search window to access the free video.

EXECUTIVE ESSENTIALS: ALSACE

The first thing you will notice about Alsatian wine is that the bottles are labeled by the grape varietals, a practice known as **"varietal labeling"**. Other regions in France label their wines by the region of origin ("appellation"), but this is not the practice in Alsace. This makes it somewhat easier for you to identify the type of wine in a bottle from Alsace as the grape is listed prominently.

It is also important to know that Alsace is really a **white wine region**, known primarily for wines from the **Gewurztraminer** and **Riesling** grapes.

ALSACE GEOGRAPHY

Alsace is located in the North of France around the city of Strasbourg. This area is located along the border with Germany and has a strong German influence and in fact grows many of the same grapes used in German wines.

ALSACE GRAPES

Gewurztraminer is a pink-colored grape known to produce pungent and extremely aromatic white wines. It is commonly produced in both sweet and dry styles.

Riesling is a German grape by origin and can produce some of the finest white wines in the world. Like Gewurztraminer, Riesling is also commonly produced in both sweet and dry styles. Also note that Alsace is actually the only region in all of France legally permitted to grow the Riesling grape.

GEWURZTRAMINER TASTING NOTES

Typical **Gewurztraminer** aromas, flavors, and characteristics:
- Lychee, peach, mango
- Ginger
- Nutmeg, allspice, cardamom
- Extremely aromatic

Gewurztraminer is commonly made in both dry and sweet styles. Be sure to clarify which variety you are ordering if it is not clear.

GEWURZTRAMINER FOOD PAIRING

Potential food pairings for **Gewurztraminer**:
- Spicy food (not heat, but spice)
- Chinese 5-spice, Indian Masala spice
- Fruits and cheeses

This wine is frequently said to be a good pairing with "Asian food". The problem is that "Asian food" is a very broad category when stated in this undifferentiated way. The more specific pairing advice you should heed is that the spicy complexity of the wine is a good match for dishes of equally exotic use of spice.

GEWURZTRAMINER BOTTLES TO KNOW

Grand Cru
The top vineyards in Alsace are designated "Grand Cru", a category you can use as a marker of quality when looking at a wine list.

RIESLING TASTING NOTES

Typical **Riesling** aromas, flavors, and characteristics:
- Citrus, apples, tropical fruit
- Petrol notes (with aging in the bottle)
- Minerals, stone
- Alsatian Riesling is typically higher in alcohol than German Riesling
- High acidity

Riesling can be made in both dry and sweet styles. Be sure to clarify which variety you are ordering if it is not clear.

RIESLING FOOD PAIRING

Potential food pairings for **Riesling**:
- Chicken, duck, goose,
- Salmon, tuna
- Chinese food, cumin, curry
- Ginger, anise

Due largely to its high acidity, dry Riesling is often praised as a very "food friendly" wine. Generally speaking, acidity in wine tends to make the flavors in food more pronounced and adds a nice crispness to the wine itself.

RIESLING BOTTLES TO KNOW

Grand Cru
The top vineyards in Alsace are designated "Grand Cru", a category you can use as a marker of quality when looking at a wine list.

EXECUTIVE SUMMARY: ALSACE

Alsace is the only region in France permitted to label grapes by the varietal, and they produce fine white wines from Gewurztraminer and Riesling. Be aware that these wines can be made dry or sweet so be sure to differentiate what you are buying so you are not surprised. If you are aiming for high quality Alsatian wine look for the Grand Cru designation.

Video Supplement: "Alsace Essentials"
www.executivewineeducation.com

Enter the video title in the search window to access the free video.

EXECUTIVE ESSENTIALS: LOIRE

The Loire Valley is known for being the home of **Sauvignon Blanc**, a white grape which does particularly well in the sub-region of Sancerre within the Loire. Another white grape called Chenin Blanc is commonly identified with the Loire region as well but we will focus our attention on Sauvignon Blanc.

LOIRE GEOGRAPHY

The Loire is the longest river in France and it passes through many vineyard areas on its way to the Atlantic.

LOIRE GRAPES

The Loire River Valley can get quite cool and its vineyards focus on white grapes suited to this climate. Pinot Noir, a red wine grape, is grown here to a limited extent as is the red grape Cabernet Franc. However, the primary grapes are the white grapes Chenin Blanc and Sauvignon Blanc and we will focus specifically on **Sauvignon Blanc** below as it is the wine from this region you are most likely to encounter.

SAUVIGNON BLANC (LOIRE) TASTING NOTES

Typical **Sauvignon Blanc** (Loire) aromas, flavors, and characteristics:
- Grapefruit, lime, melon, passion fruit
- Cut grass
- High acidity
- Light color

Sauvignon Blanc produce high acidity, crisp white wines and often has "grassy" characteristics in its aromas and flavors. This can be highly distinctive and sometimes polarizing. For some it is the signature of their favorite wine, whereas for others this can be unpleasant when strong.

SAUVIGNON BLANC (LOIRE) FOOD PAIRING

Potential food pairings for **Sauvignon Blanc** (Loire) wine:
- Chicken, pork
- Fish, shellfish
- Greek salads, Caesar salads
- Fresh herbs

This wine can be paired with a variety of foods, including white meat and fish dishes. It will pair particularly well with fresh herbs as they would complement the herbal and sometimes grassy character that is frequently observed in the wine.

LOIRE BOTTLES TO KNOW

Sancerre
Sancerre, located at the eastern end of the Loire Valley, is well known for the quality of its Sauvignon Blanc.

EXECUTIVE SUMMARY: LOIRE

The Loire Valley produces white wines from the Sauvignon Blanc and Chenin Blanc grape varieties and is best known for the quality of its Sauvignon Blanc in particular. Sauvignon Blanc is a white grape with high acidity which makes it able to be paired successfully with a variety of dishes. It is also known for its characteristic grassy aromas and flavors. The finest examples of Loire Valley Sauvignon Blanc come from the sub-region of Sancerre.

Video Supplement: "Loire Essentials"
www.executivewineeducation.com

Enter the video title in the search window to access the free video.

CHAPTER 3

ITALY

EXECUTIVE ESSENTIALS: TUSCANY

Tuscany is most closely associated with red wines made from the **Sangiovese** grape and the wines of the **Chianti** region are the best known examples. Another example of a Sangviose wine is **Brunello di Montalcino**, which is made from a clone of the Sangiovese grape grown in and around the town of Montalcino. The Brunello clone of the Sangiovese grape can produce some of the finest red wines in Italy.

Although Tuscany's wine reputation is founded on Sangiovese red wines, they also produce a relatively well known white wine from the **Vernaccia** grape.

One final point that is of interest from an executive perspective would be the category of Tuscan wine known as "Super-Tuscan". **Super-Tuscan wines** are high quality wines that are produced in Tuscany but which do not adhere to the regional traditions with respect to prescribed grapes and techniques. There are certain bottles from Tuscany that are excellent but are not Sangiovese wines or do not abide by Tuscany's wine making rules and thus cannot label themselves under Italy's more typical regional classification system.

TUSCANY GEOGRAPHY

The Tuscany region is in central Italy centered around the city of Florence.

TUSCANY GRAPES

Sangiovese is the heart of Tuscan wine, if not Italian wine overall. Many are familiar with Italian wine through their experience in drinking the red wines of Chianti, which are made from the Sangiovese grape. Sangiovese has several clones which produce other wines in the Tuscany region, the most noble of which is the Brunello grape.

Vernaccia is the most famous white grape of Tuscany. It grows throughout Italy but is best known for its wines produced around the small town of San Gimignano ("Vernaccia di San Gimignano").

SANGIOVESE (CHIANTI) TASTING NOTES

Typical **Sangiovese** (Chianti) aromas, flavors, and characteristics:
- Tart cherries, violets
- Leather, chocolate, earth, baked clay
- Bitter finish at times
- Moderate tannin structure
- High acidity

Chianti wines from the Sangiovese grape can often be a very good value for money. Their tannin structure, mouth-feel, and slightly bitter finish are distinctive and once accustomed to these wines you'll likely be able to differentiate them by these characteristics.

SANGIOVESE (CHIANTI) FOOD PAIRING

Potential food pairings for **Sangiovese** (Chianti) wine:
- Poultry, veal
- Italian pasta, pizza
- Red sauces
- Basil, oregano

Chianti is the quintessential Italian food wine to be paired with pasta, pizza, and dishes with the typical red sauces associated with Italian food.

CHIANTI (SANGIOVESE) BOTTLES TO KNOW

Chianti Classico Riserva

"Chianti" denotes that the wine is from the Chianti region and made in accordance to the rules pertaining to this region. "Chianti *Classico*" refers to a subset of the greater Chianti region, and this area is home to some of the most famous Chianti wines. Finally the "Riserva" designation in "Chianti Classico *Riserva*" indicates that the wine has spent a minimum amount of time aging in oak and has passed other more stringent quality requirements.

BRUNELLO TASTING NOTES

Typical **Brunello** aromas, flavors, and characteristics:
- Cherry, blackberry, raspberry
- Leather, violets
- Wood
- Smooth tannin structure

BRUNELLO FOOD PAIRING

Potential food pairings for **Brunello** wine:
- Grilled steak, game
- Meat sauces
- Full-flavor cheeses

Tuscany is very well known for a steak called "Bistecca alla Fiorentina" and this wine would be the perfect match for this steak. Brunello will go well with any steak or grilled meats, but if you are ordering an Italian steak you could consider pairing it with this particular Italian wine as a match made in heaven.

BRUNELLO BOTTLES TO KNOW

Biondi Santi
This family has been making Brunello wines ever since the Brunello grape was first cloned in the late 19th century. These wines are of exceptional quality and very long-aging. Some of these wines are reputed to have aged gracefully for up to 100 years.

Castello Banfi
Castello Banfi is a well-known winemaker in the Tuscany region and produces high quality Tuscan wines, including Brunello.

VERNACCIA TASTING NOTES

Typical **Vernaccia** aromas, flavors, and characteristics:
- Lime, peach
- Floral characteristics
- Oak, flint
- Almond
- Bitter finish

VERNACCIA FOOD PAIRING

Potential food pairings for **Vernaccia** wine:
- Fish, grilled seafood
- Lemon chicken
- Vegetables
- Simple pasta

Vernaccia is a fairly straightforward and drinkable white wine which would pair nicely with fish, white meat, or simple pasta dishes.

VERNACCIA BOTTLES TO KNOW

Teruzzi and Puthod
This is one of the better known winemakers for Vernaccia di San Gimignano.

Half the fun of drinking Vernaccia di San Gimignano is in visiting the picturesque town of San Gimignano in order to do so. Highly recommended.

EXECUTIVE SUMMARY: TUSCANY

Tuscany is primarily known for its red wines, and in particular the wines made in the Chianti region from the Sangiovese grape. Chianti are the best known wines in Italy and a natural pairing with Italian food. The Brunello clone of the Sangiovese grape makes some extremely high quality wines, which are known to age well and are a natural pairing for steak. Vernaccia is a white grape and produces the best known white wines of Tuscany. Finally, Tuscany is also known for its "Super-Tuscan" wines. These wines are made either with non-Tuscan grapes or non-Tuscan methods and can be of extremely high quality and international reputation.

Video Supplement: "Tuscany Essentials"
www.executivewineeducation.com

Enter the video title in the search window to access the free video.

EXECUTIVE ESSENTIALS: PIEDMONT

The Piedmont wine region is known primarily for red wines produced from the **Nebbiolo** grape, particularly from the areas of **Barolo** and **Barbaresco**. Barolo wines tend to be tannic, long-aging, and high in acid. Barbaresco wines are made from the same grape though not aged for quite as long in oak. Piedmont is also home to sparkling white wines from the Asti region, however these are less likely to hit your radar screen as an executive and I recommend simply focusing on the red Nebbiolo wines, and in particular on Barolo.

PIEDMONT GEOGRAPHY

Piedmont translates literally into "foot of the mountains" and it is located at the foothills of the Alps in northern Italy near the border with France.

PIEDMONT GRAPES

Nebbiolo is the grape used to produce the renowned red wines of Barolo and Barbaresco. This is a grape that really needs time in the bottle to soften its tannins and raise its complexity. If you are drinking a Barolo less than 10 years old then you are likely drinking it too early and you will experience an aggressively tannic wine rather than the more complex wine that Barolos become with age.

NEBBIOLO (BAROLO) TASTING NOTES

Typical **Nebbiolo** (Barolo) aromas, flavors, and characteristics:
- Tar and roses
- Dark chocolate
- Truffles and earth
- High tannin
- High acidity
- Relatively light color for such a robust red wine

Barolo begins life as a highly tannic red wine and over time it matures and opens up, gaining complexity. These wines are particularly known for displaying aromas and flavors of "tar and roses". They are also known for having a relatively light color for a wine of such high tannin and extract.

NEBBIOLO (BAROLO) FOOD PAIRING

Potential food pairings for **Nebbiolo** (Barolo) wine:
- Meats, braised beef, meaty stews
- Rich risotto or pasta
- Tomato sauces

This is a powerful wine to be paired with rich foods, proteins, and robust flavors that can stand up to it.

NEBBIOLO (BAROLO) BOTTLES TO KNOW

Cannubi Vineyards
The name "Cannubi" denotes a particular vineyard area which has actually existed even longer than the designation "Barolo". The Cannubi vineyards are located on a particular slope and grapes have been cultivated on this slope for centuries. The Nebbiolo wines produced here are known to be among the top wines of the Barolo region, and of Italy overall.

EXECUTIVE SUMMARY: PIEDMONT

Piedmont is best known for its long-aging red wines produced from the Nebbiolo grape, particularly those from the region of Barolo. Barolo is a serious wine. It is tannic and robust and meant to age for long periods in the bottle before it opens up in full maturity. To drink Barolo less than 10 years old is likely a mistake as the aromatic complexity will not yet have developed and the tannins will not have softened into the velvety texture they will later take on. The flavor and aroma profile of this wine is often described as "tar and roses".

Video Supplement: "Piedmont Essentials"
www.executivewineeducation.com

Enter the video title in the search window to access the free video.

EXECUTIVE ESSENTIALS: VENETO

Veneto is better known for the manner of its winemaking than for the specific grapes used in its wines. The most famous wine of the Veneto wine region is the red wine **Amarone della Valpolicella**. "Amarone" literally means "the great bitter" and this refers to the dry (non-sweet) style of the wine in order to distinguish it from other sweet wines also made in Valpolicella. Amarone wines are made by laying out the harvested grapes and allowing the water in the fruit to slowly evaporate in order to raise the proportion of sugar to water in the grapes. These partially dried grapes are then pressed and fermented to produce the wine.

Amarone is truly a connoisseur's wine, producing extremely full-bodied and incredibly complex red wines.

VENETO GEOGRAPHY

The Veneto region is located in northeast Italy situated between the Alps and the Adriatic Sea. As the name would suggest, the city of Venice is located within this region.

VENETO GRAPES

The grapes used to create these red wines are the **Corvina, Rondinella**, and **Molinara** grapes. However, the grapes are far less relevant to the Amarone wines of this region than are the winemaking techniques whereby the grapes are allowed to partially air-dry before they are pressed and fermented. This makes for expensive wines due to the amount of grapes required to make the final product. Given that much of the water in the grapes evaporates, the winemakers must use more fruit in order to make the same volume of wine. It is also a challenging winemaking process as during the drying process the winemakers tend to lose some fruit to rot despite their best efforts to circulate air throughout this period to mitigate this possibility.

AMARONE TASTING NOTES

Typical **Amarone** aromas, flavors, and characteristics:
- Plum, raisin, fig, prune, violets
- Leather, dark chocolate
- Soy sauce, earth
- High alcohol
- High tannin
- High pigment level
- Low acidity

Raisin flavors and concentrated fruit are especially characteristic of this robust wine.

AMARONE FOOD PAIRING

Potential food pairings for **Amarone** wine:
- Braised meats, rich stews
- Rich pastas
- Aged cheeses, parmigiano reggiano

Amarone is powerful wine and you will need to pair it with rich food, otherwise it will overwhelm your dishes and your palette.

AMARONE BOTTLES TO KNOW

Masi, Speri, Allegrini
There are 12 winemakers in Veneto who have banded together to form the "Amarone Family", a group committed to high quality standards in Amarone winemaking. Three of these winemakers to keep in mind are Masi, Speri, and Allegrini.

EXECUTIVE SUMMARY: VENETO

Veneto's wine reputation is largely built on its Amarone della Vallpolicella wines, referred to simply as "Amarone". Amarone refers to a winemaking style whereby the grapes are dried out to an extent before being pressed in order to raise the proportion of sugar to water in the fruit. All of the sugar is then fermented into alcohol resulting in powerful, high-alcohol, complex wines that tend to be expensive due to the amount of fruit and labor required in this process. This wine has somewhat of a cult following as its flavors can be complex and very powerful.

Video Supplement: "Veneto Essentials"
www.executivewineeducation.com

Enter the video title in the search window to access the free video.

CHAPTER 4

SPAIN AND GERMANY

EXECUTIVE ESSENTIALS: SPAIN

Spain produces high quality red wines, primarily from the **Tempranillo** grape. These wines are often characterized by their noticeable oak flavors which are imparted by the use of the **American oak** barrels in which they are aged before being bottled. The area of **Rioja** is the best known of the Tempranillo red wine producing regions in Spain.

Spain is also known for its Sparkling wine produced in the **Cava** wine region, particularly in the more specific area of Penedes. Simply referred to as "Cava", this wine is also often a good value and is made in a similar manner to the sparkling wines of Champagne in France.

SPAIN GEOGRAPHY

There are vineyards throughout Spain but the most internationally acclaimed wine region is Rioja, which is in northern Spain near the border with France. Its proximity to France has been a blessing and a curse. French winemakers first came to Spain from Bordeaux in numbers when a parasite known as phylloxera devastated the Bordeaux region's vineyards. Unfortunately these traveling winemakers eventually brought phylloxera with them to Spain as well. The good news is that they also brought Bordeaux winemaking techniques thus elevating Spain's red wines to a higher quality level.

The Cava wine region, known for its sparkling wines, is located in northern Spain east of Rioja near the Mediterranean Sea. The heart of Cava production is the sub-region of Penedes near the city of Barcelona.

SPAIN GRAPES

Spanish red wines are produced primarily from the **Tempranillo** grape, which is often blended with **Garnacha** (known as Grenache in France).

The Spanish sparkling wine, Cava, can be made from many grapes but it is most commonly produced from the white grapes **Macabeo**, **Xarel-lo**, and **Parellada**. These are not particularly well known grapes (internationally) and being able to recall them is less relevant in an executive context than simply understanding that Cava is Spanish sparkling wine made in a manner similar to Champagne.

TEMPRANILLO (RIOJA) TASTING NOTES

Typical **Tempranillo** (Rioja) aromas, flavors, and characteristics:
- Strawberry, cherry
- Oak, leather, tobacco
- Earth
- Vanilla

A signature trait of Rioja wine is the oak and vanilla flavors and aromas which are imparted by time spent ageing in oak. Rioja is known for its use of American oak barrels in particular. Red wines are commonly aged in either American or French oak barrels before being bottled and American oak imparts stronger flavors than French oak, particularly when using new barrels.

TEMPRANILLO (RIOJA) FOOD PAIRING

Potential food pairings for **Tempranillo** (Rioja) wine:
- Pork, grilled meat, burgers, cured meats
- Tapas, paella
- Red sauces

The wine and culinary traditions of a given region tend to evolve in parallel and can often naturally pair well together and this is the case for Rioja. Spanish Iberico ham, paella, and various tapas would go nicely with Rioja (Tempranillo) wines.

TEMPRANILLO BOTTLES TO KNOW

Rioja, Ribera del Duero, Priorat

We have focused primarily on Rioja simply because the world focuses primarily on Rioja, but note that the regions of Ribera del Duero and Priorat also produce high quality Tempranillo wines (sometimes blended with Garnacha). If you see these regions indicated on a wine list then your assumptions about Rioja wine characteristics should generally apply.

CAVA TASTING NOTES

Typical **Cava** aromas, flavors, and characteristics:
- Apple, pear, citrus
- Mushroom, earth
- Yeast, almond

Cava employs what is known as the "methode Champenoise" ("Champagne method") in making its sparkling wine. In using this method the winemaker first ferments a base wine, often blending together wines from different vintage years in order to maintain a consistent house style in the final product. Once this base wine is created it is bottled together with a dose of yeast and sugar, which is introduced in order to trigger a second fermentation in the bottles. It is this second fermentation which creates the carbon dioxide which infuses the wines under the pressure of the sealed bottles. This yeast can in turn contribute the "yeast and almond" character sometimes observed in sparkling wines made by this method.

CAVA FOOD PAIRING

Potential food pairings for **Cava** wine:
- Shrimp and shellfish
- Brie and Gouda cheeses
- Raspberries, strawberries
- Tapas, fried food

Many of these sparkling wine pairings (such as raspberries and strawberries) likely seem intuitive for sparkling wine. Note that sparkling wine can also pair well with high fat foods (such as fried food) as the wine's acidity and carbonation can cut through the fat.

CAVA BOTTLES TO KNOW

Penedes
Many of the Cava sparkling wines you will drink originate from the Penedes sub-region of Cava.

EXECUTIVE SUMMARY: SPAIN

Spain is best known for its red wines from the Rioja region which are made primarily from the Tempranillo grape. In addition to the Rioja region, the areas of Ribera del Duero and Priorat also make quality Tempranillo (or Tempranillo blend) wines. All of these red wines tend to be characterized by their noticeable oak flavors and aromas, a result of the practice of aging them in oak barrels during production.

Cava produces sparkling wines in a similar style to the Champagne wines of France. Cava tends to be good value sparkling wine and often originates from the Penedes sub-region within Cava.

Video Supplement: "Spain Essentials"
www.executivewineeducation.com

Enter the video title in the search window to access the free video.

EXECUTIVE ESSENTIALS: GERMANY

Germany is commonly associated with sweet white wines, which they do export in quantity, though its quality dry wines made from the **Riesling** grape are some of the finest white wines in the world. Riesling produces notably high acidity wines which are very well suited to pairing with food. Note that some of the highest quality Rieslings are also able to benefit from aging in the bottle, a characteristic not present in many white wines.

GERMANY GEOGRAPHY

Germany's wine regions are quite far north compared to most of the wine regions throughout the world. A northern latitude implies a shorter growing season and makes it challenging to fully ripen grapes, particularly red wine grapes. For this reason, Germany focuses on white wine grapes and utilizes vineyard sites situated on south-facing slopes to maximize exposure to sunlight. Germany's vineyards also tend to be situated near river valleys which tends to mitigate temperature swings.

GERMANY GRAPES

Riesling is the king of German wines. This white grape can withstand Germany's shorter growing season and cooler temperatures and produces food-friendly, high quality white wines. It is used to produce sweet white wines as well as dry white wines.

RIESLING TASTING NOTES

Typical **Riesling** aromas, flavors, and characteristics:
- Citrus, apples, floral
- Minerals, stone
- Petrol notes with age
- High acidity
- Often lower alcohol levels than Alsatian Riesling

Petrol may seem an odd aroma for a wine to display, but it's commonly cited in older Rieslings that have aged in the bottle. As to whether this is a positive or negative characteristic is a subject of some debate, but it is known to occur in older Rieslings including, if not especially, in those of high quality.

RIESLING FOOD PAIRING

Potential food pairings for **Riesling** wine:
- Chicken, duck, goose
- Salmon, tuna
- Chinese food, cumin, curry, Thai spice
- Ginger, anise

Due in part to its high acidity, Riesling is often praised as a very "food friendly" wine able to be paired well with a wide variety of foods. Acidity in wine tends to make the flavors in food seem more pronounced while at the same time adding a nice crispness to the wine. You may even consider Riesling when matching foods such as Chinese or Thai spiced dishes, which can be challenging to pair with wines. If the dishes have a high degree of not only spice but heat, then consider pairing a Riesling with a degree of residual sugar (a sweet, as opposed to dry, Riesling).

RIESLING BOTTLES TO KNOW

Mosel
The vineyards of Mosel-Saar-Ruwer (referred to simply as "Mosel") are particularly famous for the quality of their Riesling. These vineyards are situated along the Mosel, Saar, and Ruwer rivers and these vineyard-lined riverbanks can be quite steep and very picturesque.

EXECUTIVE SUMMARY: GERMANY

Many associate Germany with sweet white wines, but first and foremost Germany is the home of dry white Riesling, a noble white wine produced in very high quality particularly in Mosel. These wines can be drunk young, but some are also able to age gracefully in the bottle. Riesling is known to be a particularly food friendly wine due to its high acidity level.

Video Supplement: "Germany Essentials"
www.executivewineeducation.com

Enter the video title in the search window to access the free video.

CHAPTER 5

UNITED STATES

EXECUTIVE ESSENTIALS: CALIFORNIA

California, and in particular Napa Valley, has developed a reputation for very high quality red wines produced from the **Cabernet Sauvignon** grape. In fact, some of these wines are referred to as "Cult Cabernets" as a testament to their "cult" status in that they are expensive and very exclusive. In terms of quality, the finest California Cabernet Sauvignon can rival the finest Bordeaux wines of similar style (Left Bank Bordeaux, for example).

California is also known for its red **Zinfandel** wines. The Zinfandel grape thrives in California's climate and produces full-bodied, high-alcohol wines. This grape is commonly thought to be native to the United States, but that is actually a misconception and not the case.

Finally, California is also well known for quality **Chardonnay** white wines. However, California Chardonnay is typically made in a different style than Chardonnay grown in France (in Chablis, for instance).

CALIFORNIA GEOGRAPHY

The bulk of the US wine industry's production (particularly for high quality wine) comes from the state of California and the heart of California winemaking is the Napa Valley, a region just north of the city of San Francisco.

CALIFORNIA GRAPES

In the United States wines are listed by the primary grape variety in the bottle, as opposed to listing by the region of production (a common practice in Europe). In California, in order for a wine to label itself as a given grape varietal (labeling as "Cabernet Sauvignon", for example) the proportion of that grape in the bottle must be at least 75%. Winemakers may blend other grapes (not listed on the label) so long as their proportion does not exceed 25%.

The **Cabernet Sauvignon** grape traces its origin to the Bordeaux region in France, but it grows particularly well in California today. In its home in Bordeaux this grape is commonly blended with Merlot and in California this is also the case. More generally, the Cabernet Sauvignon grape produces some of the finest red wines in the world and many believe it to be the "king of grapes" when it comes to full-bodied red wines.

California has been trying for years to demonstrate that its Cabernet can rival the fine wines of Bordeaux and several blind tastings have taken place in order to pit the wines of these two regions against one another. In a famous blind tasting in 1976, known as the "Challenge of Paris", California wines famously won the majority of critical acclaim in a competition against the top red Bordeaux wines. This shocked the wine world and brought California wine onto the international stage more credibly. California has come a long way since these early tastings and it is no longer surprising to hold the fine California Cabernets in such high esteem and their price tags and lack of availability now reflect this.

Note that California Cabernet Sauvignon and California Merlot go somewhat hand in hand in that they are both Bordeaux varietals, they are often made in similar styles, and they are often blended together. California Merlot will sometimes resemble California Cabernet, but with a softer tannin structure (and may contain up to 25% Cabernet Sauvignon in any case).

The **Zinfandel** grape produces robust red wines that many feel to be "identity" wines for California and distinctly American. While Zinfandel is best known in California, this grape is genetically identical to the Primitivo grape grown in Italy. Upon investigation it was determined that Zinfandel actually traces its earlier origins back to Croatia.

Do not confuse Zinfandel ("Red Zinfandel") with *White* Zinfandel. White Zinfandel is a blush wine made from the same grape but bears little resemblance to the full bodied red wines that bear the Zinfandel name.

Chardonnay traces its roots back to France where it is the grape behind the white wines of Chablis. However, California Chardonnay tends to be different in style from the Chardonnay wines made in France. California Chardonnay has a reputation for aging in oak barrels and often picks up strong oak and vanilla character. Chablis (produced from Chardonnay grown in the Chablis region of France) tends to be "flinty and minerally" in nature and is more often not aged in oak and does not pick up such vanilla and oak flavors and aromas.

CABERNET SAUVIGNON (CALIFORNIA) TASTING NOTES

Typical **Cabernet Sauvignon** aromas, flavors, and characteristics:
- Black cherry, currant, blackberry
- Green bell pepper
- Cedar wood, tobacco
- Vanilla, mint
- High pigment levels
- High tannin

Cabernet is a full-bodied red wine with notable tannin structure, especially when drunk young. California Cabernet is known for being a bit more "fruit forward" than its Bordeaux counterparts in that you may detect stronger fruit flavors and aromas in California Cabernet than in Bordeaux wines. In many cases this generalization will not hold, but it is a widely subscribed generalization.

CABERNET SAUVIGNON (CALIFORNIA) FOOD PAIRING

Potential food pairings for **Cabernet Sauvignon** wine:
- Beef, steak
- Aged cheeses
- Red wine sauces, rich sauces
- Rosemary, sage, bay

This is a good wine to pair with beef or steak as its strong tannin structure and powerful flavor profile goes well with high-fat, high-flavor foods.

CABERNET SAUVIGNON BOTTLES TO KNOW

Stag's Leap
This is the winemaker that won first prize against the best Bordeaux reds in a blind tasting in 1976 known as the "Judgment of Paris". Stags Leap has enjoyed a reputation for very high quality Cabernet Sauvignon ever since.

Opus One
This is a joint venture between top talent in California and top talent in Bordeaux. Baron Philippe de Rothschild (of Chateau Mouton Rothschild, a first-growth Bordeaux) and Robert Mondavi (maker of the renowned Mondavi wines of California that bear his name) have joined together to make this famous Cabernet-driven, Bordeaux-style red wine.

ZINFANDEL TASTING NOTES

Typical **Zinfandel** aromas, flavors, and characteristics:
- Raspberry, blackberry, raisin
- Candied fruit, jam
- Cedar wood
- Clove, anise
- High alcohol
- High pigment
- High tannin levels

Zinfandel is a robust, spicy, high-alcohol red wine. Its fruit is often very pronounced and can come across as concentrated in its aromas and flavors displaying "raisin-like" characteristics at times.

ZINFANDEL FOOD PAIRING

Potential food pairings for **Zinfandel** wine:
- Steak, pepper steak
- Turkey
- Cajun sauce, bbq sauce
- Black pepper, garlic

Consider matching the spiciness of the wine with highly spiced or pungent foods. Spice is not to be confused with heat. If you have spicy foods with a high level of heat then reconsider pairing Zinfandel as the high alcohol levels in this wine may exacerbate the heat in the food.

I am personally fond of pairing Zinfandel with Thanksgiving turkey as I feel it pairs two American classics together, but admittedly this may be more of a sentimental pairing than a culinary pairing unless your turkey is well-spiced and highly flavored.

ZINFANDEL BOTTLES TO KNOW

Ridge, Ravenswood
Both of these winemakers are expert in making Zinfandel and do so with consistent quality levels.

CHARDONNAY TASTING NOTES

Typical **Chardonnay** aromas, flavors, and characteristics:
- Melon, peach, apricot
- Vanilla, oak
- Butter, butterscotch

Winemaking methods have a strong impact on Chardonnay wine. California Chardonnay is well known for oak flavors (imparted from time spent ageing in oak), and at times excessively so, but how you perceive this is really a matter of your preferences and palette. California Chardonnay is also known for being "buttery" in flavor and texture.

CHARDONNAY FOOD PAIRING

Potential food pairings for **Chardonnay** wine:
- Chicken, pork, turkey
- Crab, lobster, shrimp
- Cream sauce, bernaise sauce

CHARDONNAY BOTTLES TO KNOW

Montelena
This was the winning white wine in the blind tasting in 1976 known as the "Judgment of Paris". This tasting pitted California whites and reds against French counterparts and California (and Montelena specifically) came out on top to everyone's surprise.

EXECUTIVE SUMMARY: CALIFORNIA

California, and Napa Valley in particular, is home to some big red wines. Zinfandel is a robust, high-alcohol, and distinctly American red wine which thrives in California. California has also gained renown for its Cabernet Sauvignon wines which are known to rival the finest Bordeaux wines in France. Some of these California Cabernet Sauvignon wines are referred to as "Cult Cabernets" due to their price and lack of availability. Finally, California is also home to quality Chardonnay wines made in a style that tends to often display pronounced "oaky and buttery" aromas and flavors due to the winemaking style of the region.

Video Supplement: "California Essentials"
www.executivewineeducation.com

Enter the video title in the search window to access the free video.

CHAPTER 6

SOUTHERN HEMISPHERE

EXECUTIVE ESSENTIALS: AUSTRALIA

Australia produces a wide variety of wines, but it is building its reputation primarily around the **Shiraz** (known in France as Syrah) grape. This grape traces its roots back to the Rhone Valley in France but has found a perfect second home in Australia where it is producing quality red wines. The most famous, and collectable, example of Australian Shiraz can be found in the **Grange** wines of Penfolds winery.

AUSTRALIA GEOGRAPHY

The bulk of Australia's vineyards are in the southeastern area of the country where the climate is cooler and better suited to viticulture.

AUSTRALIA GRAPES

Shiraz is practically synonymous with Australian wine. Originally at home in the Rhone Valley (where it is referred to as Syrah) in France, this grape is thriving in Australia. Australia is producing many quality wines, including from other grapes, but as an executive I would advise that you associate this red grape in particular with Austrialia.

SHIRAZ TASTING NOTES

Typical **Shiraz** aromas, flavors, and characteristics:
- Raspberry, jam
- Tar, musk, chocolate
- Smoke, black pepper
- Rosemary, lavender
- High pigment
- High tannin
- High alcohol

Syrah (Shiraz) grown in the Rhone Valley in France tends to be smoky and earthy whereas Shiraz (Syrah) grown in Australia is often "jammier" showing more fruit character.

SHIRAZ FOOD PAIRING

Potential food pairings for **Shiraz** wine:
- Lamb, sausage, grilled meats
- Peppery sauces
- Pungent herbs and spices

This tends to be a big wine and you can pair it with big flavors, such as peppery sauces or pungent herbs.

SHIRAZ BOTTLES TO KNOW

Penfolds Grange
This is the bottle to know and recognize on the wine list and in conversation when it comes to high-end Australian wine. This wine first made by winemaker Max Schubert of Penfolds winery and in fact it was relatively unloved when first released. Schubert was trying to emulate the techniques he had observed in the Bordeaux region in France but initially consumers were not receptive and Penfolds asked him to discontinue production of the wine. He secretly continued to make the wine nonetheless and as the bottles from earlier years matured and demonstrated more complexity with age they were finally appreciated. Grange is now recognized as one of the finest wines in the world and an iconic bottle worth collecting.

EXECUTIVE SUMMARY: AUSTRALIA

Australia produces many quality wines, largely in the southeastern part of the country. However, its reputation is largely built on the Shiraz grape, known in its original home in the Rhone Valley (France) as Syrah. These wines can reach exceptional heights in quality, the Penfolds Grange wines being their most famous example. Grange is one of the world's most sought after bottles and is highly collectable and will improve with age.

Video Supplement: "Australia Essentials"
www.executivewineeducation.com

Enter the video title in the search window to access the free video.

EXECUTIVE ESSENTIALS: NEW ZEALAND

New Zealand has a reputation for producing some of the finest **Sauvignon Blanc** wines in the world. Sauvignon Blanc is a white grape that traces its roots back to the Loire region of France where it grows particularly well in the sub-region of Sancerre. Today New Zealand has embraced this grape to the extent that the country is known almost singularly for this wine. The area of **Marlborough** at the northern tip of the South Island is especially well known for the quality of its Sauvignon Blanc wines.

NEW ZEALAND GEOGRAPHY

There is more vineyard land on the North Island than the South Island, but the South Island is better known in terms of international reputation. On the South Island the Marlborough area, in particular, has established a shining reputation and consumers will often seek out Sauvignon Blanc wines specifically from Marlborough.

NEW ZEALAND GRAPES

The **Sauvignon Blanc** grape makes high acidity, crisp white wines often characterized by a "grassy" character.

SAUVIGNON BLANC TASTING NOTES

Typical **Sauvignon Blanc** aromas, flavors, & characteristics:
- Grapefruit, lime, melon, passion fruit
- Freshly cut grass
- High acidity
- Light color

SAUVIGNON BLANC FOOD PAIRING

Potential food pairings for **Sauvignon Blanc** wine:
- Chicken, pork
- Fish, shellfish
- Greek salad, Caesar salad
- Fresh herbs

Fresh herbs would pair very well with Sauvignon Blanc and complement the grassy character of the wine itself. A salad with fresh herbs together with a cold Sauvignon Blanc on a hot day would be a perfect combination.

SAUVIGNON BLANC BOTTLES TO KNOW

Cloudy Bay
This wine is well known in wine circles as an example of New Zealand's finest Sauvignon Blanc. If your clients recognize one wine from New Zealand it is likely this bottle from the Marlborough region.

Marlborough Region
If you are selecting from among different New Zealand Sauvignon Blanc, simply look for this region on the label. Marlborough is known for its fine Sauvignon Blanc, and while this generalization won't always hold true it is still a pretty good bet.

EXECUTIVE SUMMARY: NEW ZEALAND

New Zealand Sauvignon Blanc is recognized the world over. The grape has roots back to the Loire region in France but is now quite at home in New Zealand. This grape produces crisp white wines with high acidity and a distinct "grassy" character. Sauvignon Blanc is particularly reputable in the Marlborough region on the North Island, the most famous example being the bottles from winemaker Cloudy Bay.

Video Supplement: "New Zealand Essentials"
www.executivewineeducation.com

Enter the video title in the search window to access the free video.

EXECUTIVE ESSENTIALS: ARGENTINA

Argentina has placed its focus on the red wines of **Malbec**, a grape that traces its roots back to the Bordeaux region in France. Malbec is one of the 5 grapes (together with Cabernet Sauvignon, Merlot, Cabernet Franc, and Petit Verdot) permitted to be used in the blend that creates the famous red wines of Bordeaux.

Today Malbec is not widely grown in Bordeaux other than in an area called Cahors where it is the grape responsible for the "black wines of Cahors", so called due to the dark color of the Malbec grape. In fact, this dark color is one of the key aspects the grape is known to impart in the Bordeaux blend when used. Malbec now sees its greatest heights in Argentina, particularly in the Mendoza wine region, and it is the most important grape in the Argentine wine industry.

While Argentina is overwhelmingly known for its red (largely Malbec) wines, it is also known for a white wine produced from the **Torrontes** grape which grows primarily in the Salta wine region north of Mendoza.

ARGENTINA GEOGRAPHY

Argentina's geography is quite dramatic. The Andes mountains can be seen in the background of the vineyards, their white capped peaks providing a beautiful and stark contrast to the greenery of the vines. The snowmelt runoff from the Andes mountains serves as a source of irrigation for the vines in Argentina, especially in Mendoza, the heart of Argentina's wine production.

ARGENTINA GRAPES

Malbec is native to Bordeaux and one of the 5 grapes in the Bordeaux blend. This grape is notable for its dark color. It produces dark, "inky" wines and has a moderate tannin structure somewhat similar in character to the more widely familiar Merlot grape (also a Bordeaux varietal).

The **Torrontes** grape is grown primarily in Salta and produces aromatic whites. In this respect its character can be likened to the Viognier wines of the Northern Rhone which are likewise known for their aromatic perfume.

MALBEC TASTING NOTES

Typical **Malbec** aromas, flavors, and characteristics:
- Plum, blackberry, raisin
- Chocolate, earth
- Violets, black pepper
- Dark pigment
- Moderate tannin structure

This wine is often blended with a degree of Cabernet Sauvignon which lends greater tannin structure to the wine in the resulting blend.

MALBEC FOOD PAIRING

Potential food pairings for **Malbec** wine:
- Steak, sausage, lamb shank, braised meat
- Bolognese sauce
- Garlic

Malbec can stand up well to beef. The steaks and grilled meats for which Argentina is well renowned would be a good pairing for this wine.

MALBEC BOTTLES TO KNOW

Catena
The Catena wines are widely distributed (exported) and the winery produces a range of wines, some of which very high quality. Nicolas Catena is also recognized as one of the leading figures in Argentina's wine industry.

TORRONTES TASTING NOTES

Typical **Torrontes** aromas, flavors, and characteristics:
- Peach, orange, lychee, honeysuckle
- Jasmine
- Floral and highly aromatic

TORRONTES FOOD PAIRING

Potential food pairings for **Torrontes** wine:
- Grilled chicken
- Seafood
- Pizza
- Spicy food, Thai food, Vietnamese food
- Goat cheese

This wine, with its highly floral character, can pair well with certain foods that are highly spiced (not necessarily "hot", but spiced) such as Thai and Vietnamese cuisine.

TORRONTES BOTTLES TO KNOW

Salta
Torrontes' spiritual home is in the Salta region, north of the Mendoza wine region.

EXECUTIVE SUMMARY: ARGENTINA

Argentina has undergone a real explosion in its wine industry in terms of availability, recognition, and quality. Many highly skilled winemakers (some flying in from elsewhere to try their craft in Argentina) are working to produce quality Malbec making it an exciting grape with a perfectly suited home in the Mendoza region. This grape produces dark colored and rich wines, able to be paired with steak and well suited to the beef that Argentina is equally known for.

Torrontes is an interesting and floral white wine from the Salta region north of Mendoza and it is a suitable complement to aromatically spiced foods.

Video Supplement: "Argentina Essentials"
www.executivewineeducation.com

Enter the video title in the search window to access the free video.

EXECUTIVE ESSENTIALS: CHILE

Chile has established a reputation for Cabernet Sauvignon and Merlot of respectable quality and value for money. These are both red Bordeaux grapes and Chile is competent in producing them, but they are not the most interesting wines in Chile. Chile's most interesting wine comes from the **Carmenere** grape which also traces its roots back to Bordeaux, but with even deeper history than the 5 red Bordeaux grapes (Cabernet Sauvignon, Merlot, Cabernet Franc, Petit Verdot, and Malbec) known for producing the red Bordeaux blend.

CHILE GEOGRAPHY

Chile is a long, narrow sliver of land lodged between the Andes Mountains and the Pacific Ocean and its vineyards are positioned around the river valleys that make their way from the Andes to the ocean.

CHILE GRAPES

The **Carmenere** grape played a leading role in the Bordeaux region of France before any of the 5 traditional red Bordeaux grapes (Cabernet Sauvignon, Merlot, Cabernet Franc, Petit Verdot, and Malbec) were cultivated. However, it was devastated by the Phylloxera parasite in 1867 (in an infamous wave of Phylloxera that destroyed many of Europe's vineyards) and virtually disappeared from the region and was thought to have gone extinct. It later turned up in Chile where it was mistakenly thought to be Merlot until its true identity was later revealed. Today it grows extremely well in Chile and has "signature grape" status in the country.

CARMENERE TASTING NOTES

Typical **Carmenere** aromas, flavors, and characteristics:
- Raspberry, blackberry
- Green bell pepper
- Chocolate, coffee, tobacco
- Oak, vanilla
- Dark pigment
- Moderate tannin structure

This wine has similar tannin structure to Merlot and was originally mistaken for the Merlot grape before its identity was accurately identified.

CARMENERE FOOD PAIRING

Potential food pairings for **Carmenere** wine:
- Spicy (not necessarily "hot") meat dishes
- Lamb, duck, rabbit, stews
- Dark chocolate
- Rosemary, garlic

CARMENERE BOTTLES TO KNOW

Caliterra
Caliterra is one of the better known producers of quality Carmenere wines.

EXECUTIVE SUMMARY: CHILE

Chile has proven itself capable of growing many grapes and produces a wide variety of wines, particularly reds. However, its most interesting grape is Carmenere, a red Bordeaux grape thought to have been lost forever but which has now emerged on the other side of the world and can produce excellent full-bodied red wines.

Video Supplement: "Chile Essentials"
www.executivewineeducation.com

Enter the video title in the search window to access the free video.

EXECUTIVE ESSENTIALS: SOUTH AFRICA

South Africa and the areas around Capetown have a wine history dating back to the mid-1600s when representatives of the Dutch East India Company first planted grapes (thought to ward off scurvy) in this area. However, more recently South Africa's wine history has been marred by the period of Apartheid during which time a world-wide embargo challenged the economy. In the nineties this lifted and South Africa's wine industry has been on a forward march ever since. Today South Africa produces a variety of wines but is best known for **Pinotage**, a grape created in Stellenbosch University by crossing the Pinot Noir and Cinsault grapes.

SOUTH AFRICA GEOGRAPHY

South Africa is located at the Southernmost tip of the African continent and its wine regions are clustered near Capetown. The most famous regions in South Africa are Stellenbosch and Paarl.

SOUTH AFRICA GRAPES

South Africa is undergoing a quality revolution whereby their vineyard land and wine quality is being improved and they are making strides in various grapes. They are known for growing the white grape Chenin Blanc, which is known locally in South Africa as "Steen". They are also known for the red grape **Pinotage**, a grape nearly unique to South Africa which was created by crossing the Pinot Noir (a grape originally from Burgundy in France) with Cinsault (a grape originally from the Rhone Valley in France). The resulting red wine ironically does not bear much resemblance to either of its constituent parts.

PINOTAGE TASTING NOTES

Typical **Pinotage** aromas, flavors, and characteristics:
- Tropical fruit
- Cherry, plum, berry
- Smoky, earthy
- High tannin

This grape can produce quality wine, but it is prone to potentially wide variability in quality.

PINOTAGE FOOD PAIRING

Potential food pairings for **Pinotage** wine:
- Turkey, duck
- Pulled pork, chilli, pizza
- Aged cheeses
- Spicy (not necessarily "hot") food

SOUTH AFRICA BOTTLES TO KNOW

Stellenbosch Region
Stellenbosch is one of South Africa's best known wine regions and is where the Pinotage grape was first created in Stellenbosch University.

EXECUTIVE SUMMARY: SOUTH AFRICA

South Africa has had a wine history ever since the Dutch East India Company began growing grapes near Capetown, but its wine history has been discontinuous due to the economic challenges of Apartheid. Since the end of Apartheid, and the lifting of economic sanctions, South Africa's wine industry has been moving forward. They have been replanting vineyards and emphasizing quality improvements. South Africa is also home to a unique grape, Pinotage, which was truly born in the country as a cross between the Pinot Noir and Cinsault grapes. This grape makes interesting and unique wine but be aware that its quality can be variable and unpredictable.

Video Supplement: "South Africa Essentials"
www.executivewineeducation.com

Enter the video title in the search window to access the free video.

CHAPTER 7

FOUNDATIONS AND ETIQUETTE

CORKS AND CLOSURES

Wine closures are typically taken for granted but there are a few points relating to closures that are important for you to know. You should understand the different types of closures together with their advantages and disadvantages. You should also understand a particular wine flaw known as "cork taint" and what causes this problem.

Natural Cork

Natural cork come from the bark of a particular type of oak tree and in this respect it is "natural" as the name would suggest. Many consider natural cork to be the most (if not only) appropriate closure for a wine bottle. Some go even further and inject a bit of snobbery into the assessment, shunning other closures as being of a lower class.

Cork is an excellent closure and swells to fit the entrance of the wine bottle very effectively thus protecting the wine from oxygen. However cork does have one critical vulnerability which has resulted in a search for different forms of closure. Cork is vulnerable to a phenomenon known as "cork taint". When someone indicates that a wine is "corked", this is what they are referring to. Some believe that cork taint is caused by a leaky cork, while others believe it refers to when bits of cork crumble into the wine and affect the flavors of the wine. Neither is the case.

Cork taint is a wine flaw caused by the presence of the chemical compound trichloroanisole, commonly referred to as "TCA". TCA is associated with natural cork, but can also form in the presence of bleach and cleaning solutions. When present in the wine this compound can be detected in very low concentrations and its effects are insidious and can ruin (or degrade) what would otherwise be good wine.

Cork taint imparts a scent of "wet cardboard" or even "wet dog" when strong. When subtle, it dulls the fruit of a wine making it less interesting. It is difficult to assess the rate of incidence of this problem, but it is estimated that cork taint (TCA) is present in detectable levels in roughly of 1% of wines. That's a lot of wine and this issue provides a motive to search for alternative means of closure. The main alternatives to natural cork are synthetic corks and screw caps.

Synthetic Cork

Synthetic corks are an attempt to circumvent the vulnerability of natural cork to cork taint. They are created from plastic compounds and winemakers are experimenting with different variations of such closures. There are concerns that some of these closures appear to allow oxygen to pass into the bottle over time and that they may not be appropriate for longer-aging wines. There are also concerns that they could impart chemical scents and aromas into the wine.

Screw Caps

A screw cap is simply a screw-on cap for wine bottles, as the name would suggest. Screw caps were initially shunned as a marker of a cheap wine with consumers preferring the romantic quality of natural cork to the seemingly cheaper or more industrial appearance of screw caps. However in some regions the screw cap is being embraced as a perfectly practical solution, particularly for white wines. In Australia the use of screw caps is common at this writing.

Screw caps are under scrutiny over concerns that they face the opposite weakness of synthetic cork. While synthetic cork may potentially allow oxygen to transfer into the bottle at a harmful rate (given enough time), screw caps don't allow oxygen to enter the bottle at all. Natural cork is not completely impermeable and oxygen does transfer through over time, but at a very slow and controlled rate. For longer-aging wines there are concerns that this complete absence of oxygen transfer through the screw cap may have adverse effects on the aging process and may prevent the wines from achieving greater heights of complexity with time in the cellar.

We show and discuss the different closures on our website: www.executivewineeducation.com

Enter "Corks and Closures" in the search window to access the free video.

OPENING WINE

Particularly if you are going to entertain or host a dinner party, you will need to understand how to open a bottle of wine in a skillful manner. If you end up punching the cork into the bottle you risk splashing wine on yourself and your guests. If the cork breaks you risk crumbling cork into the bottle. And if you generally struggle to muscle the cork out of the bottle with brute force you risk appearing as though you've never done this before. It's worth ensuring that you are skilled at opening wine in a relatively effortless and graceful manner.

There are many different tools available for opening wine. Some are mechanical and some are electronic. Some are simple and some are highly complex. I would recommend learning how to use one simple device which is fairly ubiquitous, namely the "waiter's friend". If you are expert at using an electronic or more complex wine opener then you risk that you will be clumsy when not opening wine in your own home with the support of this tool.

The waiter's friend comes with a small fold-out knife, which is used to remove the foil cap. Be sure to cut the foil just beneath the wine bottle's drip-rim, rather than removing it entirely.

Then you should open the corkscrew and screw it into the cork. This will take a bit of practice. If you do not screw it in deep enough then you risk breaking the cork when you remove it. If you screw in too far you risk penetrating the bottom of the cork and dropping cork into the wine. All things considered the latter is a better outcome than the former, so err on the side of screwing the corkscrew in too far.

There is a cantilever device that swings out of the side of the waiter's friend which you need to rest on the mouth of the bottle. Then with a smooth upward motion, simply lift the cork up and out relying on the mechanical advantage of the lever to support you. As the final portion of the cork releases from the bottle you may want to slow down slightly to ensure you do not splash any wine on yourself or your guests at the final stage.

You can see the full opening process demonstrated on our website: www.executivewineeducation.com

Enter "Opening Wine" in the search window to access the free video.

DECANTING WINE

To understand decanting you must first understand the process referred to as "breathing". As wine is exposed to oxygen its character changes and this oxidation of the wine is known as "breathing". The breathing process is of particular benefit to tannic red wines, and once a full-bodied red wine is opened the process begins immediately. If you drink a full-bodied, tannic wine you will notice that the characteristics of the wine change noticeably as the wine oxidizes. The tannins will soften and wines that begin rather bitter and shy will open up to reveal softer textures and more complex aromas and flavors. In some instances it is interesting to see a wine evolve and change over the course of an evening as it continues to breathe.

For tannic red wines, there is an optimal amount of breathing (oxidation) required in order to bring the wine to its peak state. Of course, if a wine breathes for too long it turns into vinegar so naturally there is a limit to the process. More tannic wines and younger red wines, which tend to display more tannin, require more time breathing in order to be at their best.

If you leave a wine in its bottle then there is actually very little surface area exposed to the air and the wine will not breathe effectively. Left in the bottle, wine will breathe a little but not much. A better approach would be to open the bottle and then pour a few glasses, thus allowing greater surface area exposure to oxygen. An even more effective method is what is known as decanting.

A decanter is a glass vessel used to hold wine in order to promote effective breathing through greater exposure to oxygen. Decanters are also a beautiful way to pay respect to an important bottle as you showcase the wine.

To decant the wine, you simply open the bottle and slowly pour the wine into the decanter allowing all of the wine to come in contact with the air. If you are decanting an older wine there may be a small amount of sediment in the bottom of the bottle. This is to be expected and perfectly normal. As you pour your wine into the decanter, if you see such sediment then leave it behind in the wine bottle. Decanting can thus help to separate off this sediment from the rest of the wine.

Highly tannic wines will improve with roughly an hour of breathing in the decanter prior to drinking. This timing is only a guideline and each wine will evolve differently as it breathes. For older wines, the decanter is a fine method of separating off sediment (which tends to be more pronounced in older wines), but take care not to allow older wines to breathe for too long as they may move past their peak rather quickly. Younger wines will benefit from longer exposure to oxygen, which will soften their young tannins.

You can see the decanting process demonstrated on our website: www.executivewineeducation.com

Enter "Decanting Wine" in the search window to access the free video.

WINE GLASSES

Having a high quality wine glass makes a big difference in your ability to appreciate a fine wine. Likewise, having glasses designed specifically for the type of wine you are drinking is also important in order to emphasize certain desirable characteristics of the wine. Wine enthusiasts will immediately recognize and appreciate having quality stemware. Clients and colleagues less familiar may not have a nuanced appreciation of their glasses, but they will experience the difference on some level.

If you intend to serve wine in your home it is worthwhile to invest in at least 3 sets of glasses: Bordeaux red wine glasses, white wine glasses, and Champagne flutes. If you intend to entertain clients and colleagues then invest in a brand such as Riedel. Riedel is an Austrian glassmaker specializing in beautiful, simple stemware which is purpose-built to bring out the best in your wines.

Red Wine Glasses
Red wine glasses have large bowls to allow for greater surface area exposure to oxygen. The tannins in red wine will soften and develop into subtle aromas with such exposure and your glass should support this. Large bowls are also nice for swirling in the glass which further oxidizes the wine and also allows you to bring more aromas from the wine to your nose. The "Bordeaux glass" is a common style of red wine glass and has these traits.

White Wine Glasses

White wine glasses will tend to be narrower than red wine glasses. It is not necessary to oxidize white wine, and having less surface area also helps to maintain the cooler ideal serving temperature of the wine.

Sparkling Wine Glasses

Sparkling wine glasses are tall and slender. This shape allows less surface area than either red or white wine glasses and serves to maintain a cool temperature. Having less surface area exposure also helps to slow the escape of carbon-dioxide bubbles in the wine. This tall, slender glass is commonly known as a "Champagne flute".

You can see a discussion of the different wine glasses on our website: www.executivewineeducation.com

Enter "Wine Glasses" in the search window to access the free video.

CHAPTER 8

CONNECTING WITH WINE

Before we discuss how to connect more closely with wine, and with others through wine, let's turn our attention to the wine snob.

There is no uglier animal on the planet than the wine snob. The wine snob is rarely satisfied with a given wine, often holding the belief that they have higher standards and thus should rarely be impressed. Their wine knowledge is used primarily to demonstrate superiority and status. When drinking "pedestrian" wine their demeanor seems to imply that you too would be unimpressed if you only had access to the same wealth of wine information and an equally sophisticated palate.

This is ugly.

In fact, it's so ugly that the risk of appearing anything like this is probably a deterrent for many who would otherwise be interested in engaging more in the learning experience wine can offer. It's a waste of time to crusade against wine snobbery. It's too rampant and these animals are among us and unfortunately here to stay. I recommend to engage in the fantastic learning experience wine has to offer but to be vigilant about not treading anywhere near this repugnant status.

Wine can connect you to different geographies, cultures, and individuals and is fundamental to the culinary arts. Even simple wine can be reflective of the earth, climate and people of a given location and its history. It is true that there are flawed wines in the world and we don't have to enjoy them, and of course we are all entitled to preferences. But the indignation that a wine snob displays when tasting a wine that does not please their palette is often simply a misguided, small-minded reaction. Recognize wines for what they are, namely a demonstration of culture, agriculture and craftsmanship.

When you experience wine with an open mind, you open yourself up to wonderful channels for appreciation and understanding. As you continue your learning experience in wine you may wish to consider wine tourism, wine tastings, and wine clubs as a means of taking the experience further.

Wine Tourism

Wine tourism can be as simple as a day-trip to a local winery or a grand tour of the various wine regions of France. Either way, you learn about local traditions and gain a great sense of place through such experiences. When you tour a vineyard and taste a region's wines you are literally drinking the content of the regional culture and craftsmanship. When you pair that wine with the local food you also gain greater understanding of how the wine and culinary cultures evolved together, and they always do. This is an intimate experience and brings you closer to the world and the people who live in it.

In a professional context this understanding can bring you remarkable sources of rapport with individuals from different cultures. Nothing pulls the heartstrings quite like food and wine, and in particular the food and wine of "home".

Wine Tastings

Wine tastings can bring you many of the benefits of wine tourism, without your having to leave your city. If you search the internet for tastings in your local area I think you'll be surprised to see how frequent and accessible wine tastings have become. Tastings can be based on themes, grapes, regions, or even cuisine.

These tastings are a great source of learning. They are also a great means of networking. I have made several new acquaintances at such events and our common ground was a shared intellectual interest in wine. Tastings provide you with easy conversation in a relaxed environment and as long as you can spot and avoid the wine snob in the room (unfortunately, he may be there), you'll likely form new relationships and enhance your network.

Wine Clubs

My wife and I now participate in a wine tasting club together with friends and colleagues and we've truly enjoyed the experience. We continue to add new members to the group and the only criteria is that they are interested in wine and that they don't take wine, or themselves, too seriously. Each member takes turn hosting a wine tasting as we rotate "hosting-evenings" to a different host every few months.

The host for a given evening has free reign to build a theme for the rest of the group and we have dinner together as well. This allows for learning and a degree of creativity. It is also a great way to build relationships.

We have enjoyed blind tastings (in which the identity of bottles is not revealed), vertical tastings (wines from the same producer across different vintage years), and tastings from lesser-known wine regions. We currently live in Singapore and have even held an Asian wine tasting evening at which we tasted wines from Japan, India, Thailand, and Myanmar. Why not?

Wine education will continue to enhance your life whether through wine tourism, wine tastings, wine clubs, or simply during dinner at home. It is also highly relevant to your professional life. You will be in situations throughout your career where you will be able to use wine to connect with others. You'll also find yourself in situations where you'll be expected to order wine or pair wines with food. Finally, you will also be in situations where others will have ordered wine and in such instances a little knowledge of certain iconic bottles will give you greater context for understanding these gestures. Connecting with wine, and with others through wine, can raise your level of executive refinement but you want to avoid becoming the wine snob at all costs. As an executive, you don't need to know everything about wine, but you should certainly be aware of the essentials.

ABOUT THE AUTHOR

R. Sean Cochran is co-founder of Executive Wine Education, a group that creates training for corporate executives seeking to achieve a higher level of wine proficiency. Sean has over 15 years of financial services experience and is currently a Managing Director in a global financial institution. Sean holds an MBA in Finance and Economics from the Columbia Business School and is a Certified Financial Planner (CFP®) as well as a Certified Specialist of Wine (CSW) with the Society of Wine Educators.

Made in the USA
Lexington, KY
19 October 2014